Why is Snow so White?

Why is Snow so White?

F. H. Low-Beer

QUARRY PRESS

The publisher gratefully acknowledges
the financial assistance of The Canada Council,
the Department of Communications, the Ontario Arts
Council, and the Ontario Publishing Centre.

Canadian Cataloguing in Publication Data
Low-Beer, F. H. (Frank H.)
    Why is snow so white?
Poems.
ISBN 1-55082-057-5

I. Title.

PS8573.0883W49 1992   C811'.54   C92-090628-1
PR9199.3.L69W49 1992

Cover Photograph by F. H. Low-Beer.
Design by Susan Hannah.

Printed and bound in Canada
by Best-Gagné, Toronto, Ontario.

Published by *Quarry Press, Inc.*
P.O. Box 1061, Kingston, Ontario K7L 4Y5

for Sandra

Contents

Why Is Snow So White?

Why is snow so white
that simple dimension
patched against
the sooty clouds;
why do crows flap
from branch to branch
continuously
or worry the flight of
eagles and why
the platter of the
sea is tilted up
like empty pewter;
why is snow so white?

Edward Curtis

Upright in the prows
figures sway
beasts weaving with
the chant, beating
huge wings to the
waves crashing
beyond the headland
jagged with broken firs;
bear, wolf and raven
chanting and weaving,
clawing the mist,
wings beating to the
paddles, beating to
the waiting drums,
to the gaps between
the firs, to the gaps
between the beaks on
brooding poles set
before the curtain of
soft cedar and hard fir,
brooding over the
littered beach.

The paddles stop
the dugouts drift
over the rising pebbles,
the chant stops,
a raven weaves between
the firs, wings fretted
like the ferns beneath,
fine like the plaited
roots of spruce and
hemlock dyed with wolf moss,
fine as the pebbled beach
silent as the moss,
soft as the brown faces —
the prows touch the
gentle curve of stones,
figures upright
on the poles.

Sub Specie
(b. 1632)

Prisoners of Delft
captives of dreams
of palest blue,
past and beyond
caught in the
instance of a pearl,
maid and her room
one in the silence of
their common fate;
was your glow
seen by a passing
lens grinder?

Mouse

Mouse, why do I
fear you so
while you go about
your business
in my kitchen?
We dodge each other
you and I.
We run by each other
with our eyes shut,
you and I.
In your innocence
you are clever
and avoid my poison,
my ugly vicious bait,
red oily cheese
powdered white
to rid me
of your shadow
set at the corners
of my vision,
Don't you,
can't you see
you simply
must not be
in this world
of mine?

Bangalore

If one can pinpoint promise
it is when willows open
and the larch goes green
while trunks of beeches
dap and mottle in the sun.
Promise must mean less
in Bangalore than here
in this cool park.
I stare at the bronze square
at my feet thirteen
years after he did it.
I stare at the years
and the spaces
but not at him.
Now when willows make
all things possible but him
now, when he did it.

Larch

From below you can see
the uppermost branches
poking over the ridge.
Up the last pitch the
tree disappears altogether;
breath comes hard after
eighty years as scarred
skis adequate to
attain the trunk
cut into the dull snow.
Then all is crystal as
sun and tree appear
together in a brilliant marriage.
The mark reached
it is not necessary
to advance further into
that dazzling expanse,
enough to rest and
breathe and stand beside
the black branches
and wonder why each twig
so bare so brittle
so seeming dead
can give support.
Is it the comfort of
shared endurance, of
cold restraint, or
the green within?

Han Piece

The Chinese knew
the straight line
softened, satisfies;
the rectilinear gaze
from the straight eyes
grey like a goddess
bathing the new
flesh held at the breast
reflects and rereflects
from face to face
diffuses to a glow,
the counterpart
to this bronze finial.

3rd Class to the Simplon

Through the slow woods
grey with restraint
beech gives way to pine
and peach to cherry
wasting its reckless seed;
black vines order
the distance, the weight
of mountains melting.

Dr. No

Paradoxes crumble in the street
Criteria by caprice are ruled
Truth slips through a plastic clarity
Greyheads and fools drop to all fours
and sigh a last lament;
No immaculate conceptions
in *this* firmament!

Purcells

Far below
crouched in the rubble
lies the camp.
The valley twists up
through fir, then spruce
and larch to scrub.
Telltale willows mark
gullies ravaged by slides
that drop into the
swirling white;
not a softening impulse
except the snow,
the relentless snow that
blurs the puny scrub,
the deserted shaft,
the refuse heaps —
a winter absolution.
Somewhere above
the ice groans.

Graves

From scattered stones
the telling lines
hang in the air,
reverberate
and settle into
common speech;
a cloying guilt
dogs ears
and eyes;
yet it is sweet
to find the world
fulfilling
the forms of mind.

Swallow

Fluttering
to find the nest
is the heart

Coast Crossover

Like Tartar cheekbones
in a Slav heroine
the great firs tiered,
the sweep of arms
winged up, ragged
in their age, caught
symmetries formed of an
undistinguished youth —
speak of the East;
while in their shade
the slender trunks of
maple vines play out
sisterly origins as if
recoiling from the
cream flecked growth.

Easter Sunday

The range expands in slow waves
and rolls against the mounting clouds
dappling the high snows — below
greys impose on green Corot taught;
the meadowlark, a sort of thrush,
traces its arabesque across
the pale spring continuum;
a rock face in a spasm of sun
sends back a pastoral bleat
confirmed by shifting white
tended by a Sioux as right
as any Basque or Provençal.
And sage so strangely new
hides pillows of phlox —
five varieties found underfoot
that peep out mauve and rose
and some so white it looks like quartz,
and purple penstemon
and other recognizable sorts
all in their proper places.

Below Annapurna

Thatch turns to tin;
let the laced walls
stand shielding the
velvet paths
rubbed by shuffling feet
now bruised by a
whine that
drowns cockcrow and bell
in the still
blossomed air.

Dogwood in a Pennsylvania Hollow

Green, green the bend in the river
yet not the river but the
violet studded meadow, green
under the tear stained bank.

Waiting for the Nightingale

It is time to turn
thoughts to account –
the rain provides the
points to plot
a strategy – the rain
like fingers on a wall
counts out the
creases in the skin.
Only a crow
appears above the
lopped olives,
senseless limbs
stand about
aimlessly
supporting a
confusion of growth
against the line of
cypresses missing
a tooth here and there
waiting to be counted.

Meconopsis Baileyi

Pluck every blossom off
or you will lose the plant
she warned. Three years
we watched the hairy stem
twist up like any ordinary
poppy. At last the pods
appeared their secret shut –
perhaps we could allow
one bloom – Lot's wife forgotten;
blue silk unfurled, a jewelled
butterfly, a pharaoh's gown,
a mirror dusted gold from Mars.
How must the saffron monks have gasped
to see this artifice glow in the thin air.

Myth

Beware the
shifting sailor
and his wiles
as he coasts
among the isles
of inspiration
(his of course)
which he may scan
or take by force
to abandon
for another prize;
be forewarned
his strength
depends upon
a change of guise.

Your eager eye
no, to be fair
your mere presence
makes of me an image.
Why, your net of names
does cast a spell
of substance as tight
as any definition;
use, I fear,
reigns not only there
but here where turtles frown
and tigers sing.

Reno

Standing in lines
a race drops
words in slots;
sometimes before
they run out
the bells line up and out comes
a rush of love,
meaning manufactured
on the spot,
something to live on
for a while and
feed back in
one's very own machine.

Done Weeding

Innocent as
a fresh face
plain earth
sets off the stalks

Zinnias

A balloon crosses the Atlantic
settling in a French field
the yellow grain
bathed in the evening
the sound of distant shouting –
a hang-glider lifts off
a green hill
the waxen dreams of solitude –
not possible like the glow
outside the window
of petals burning their hearts out
in colours beyond words,
not possible.

Summer Apples

August heat
surrounds the
pale and heavy
apples, those
still green are
cooler, harder
to the touch;
You climb,
you stretch an
arm and leg
to cut a brown
diagonal through
green clusters;
their scent mixes with yours
as you stoop
to place
three apples
in my
waiting hands.

I feel their
cool waxed
weight,
I feel your
calf against
my arm,
and under
those pale skins
stretched over
momentary worlds
I see, smaller
than the specks
that mark
your arm,
mere points
distributed
evenly, then fade
at the lower poles
as stars do
in a morning sky.

The Concert at Sundown

Shadow threaten to overcome
the grass and blunt the
pricks of thought, links fail,
the mind coagulates, yet
still the strings play
spilling their harmless fluff;
the afterglow of summer
comes to the eyes undiminished:
the spikes of blue, the
lineage of the ancient rose,
the fretted peony, the
dented pentagon of phlox, all
layered beyond counting,
beyond the will to count.

Poem

The gull wing
laps the eve
of sleep
whispering
into a
night ear
tidings of
summer gloom,
whimsy so
softly lapped
that reeds do
register
a change of mood
with a mere
sigh of protest.

Crystals

Crystals emerge from the brine
each edge a distinction
sharpened until it cracks;
then enquiry melts
the steaming structure and the
whole mess slips
back into the sea.

Cascades

The ever
protected
wilderness area
of never being
able
to know
why
piano keys
play on your
soul.

Surfaces

Dead calm but for the pattern
woven by the wind, the tapestry
reforming the innocent lagoon,
the screen manipulated by
a whisper. Perhaps it was the
blue or perhaps the shimmer
of distant cities that would be
ravaged and forgot; or perhaps
nature's decadence — three
dying firs, seedlings when paint
was put upon the canvas, that
led me to the elders.

Yet it is not Susanna that
sparks the tinder but a
heightened flame surprised
to find itself displayed in
that great gallery — a panoply
spread front and back
of goings-on we grope to name —
there, quite as they've always been.

It is the surveyed commonality of
spread and not the flame that is
the testimony to a thing as much
as any stick or twinge.
And so the eyeing elders
led me to another canvas
locked in an attic, a ghostly counter
to that golden face, daubed
with what adds up.

The Gooseberry

He stoops to pull the vines
that choke the berrybush
the flowers mock him
sickly white, the thorns stare up
the black plum will not bear again.
It is too much for an old man,
the August tangle hides a rusty fork —
if only winter would clear all away.
High up a graft has taken,
a small green apple dangles.

On the Giving of a Telescope

Unless observation has a sense
that subtly flows into the thing observed –
as when the vastness of the moon is first
revealed
and awe melts into alien skin –
then perception fattens not the thing
perceived
so bricks are bricks and spoons are rust.
Yet there are some whose eye is fire:
stay ever so –
you need no lens to make mere matter glow
the hidden heart of common things
cries out.
A courtyard giving on to Delft
confounds the dust with brilliance
when you do look.

Figaro

Cinque, dieci, venti –
cubits enough for a wedding bed –
open and sustain a performance
to frame the inner flux;
for if there is such stuff,
it culls what it conceives –
compares, measures and counts.

Early on Pitt Lake

Black gives way to vision –
slowly above a still neutrality
the lake lifts its face
to an unseen partner,
trees walk into consciousness;
then white at lakesend
the one assertion against which
other things are set;
nothing speaks but change
no whiff of essence
cloys the borderless expanse;
breathe
before that touch of pink
turns promise overripe.

Near Prince Albert

Black strings weave crazily
fouling the evening,
resolve into computer dots
on the vast screen,
then rushing wings
necks craning to a
blind determination;
the rolling stubble
pricked by a red tower
makes do for Chartres or Bourges.

The Splash of Oars

The splash of oars
on an empty sea
loves as many
and as meaningful
sound in the ear;
on a curving beach
an exile summons
an image
from the inland sea
to serve both sides
of a lacquered screen;
all that echoes
is a distant splash.

Early Evening

Silver paring
unanswered question
hanging

Ruins by Indirection

The ball sails over
and lands downfield
the mare leaps
forward –
make that ball
settle!
I wheel and see the palms
beyond the posts
neat squares of trunks
majestic rows
of columns marching
lotus crowned,
a crumbling roof,
Karnak,
Claude,
the last sun on the dunes –
the wastes, the wastes.

Quan Jar

Fat speckled
fish you
are so gay
as you
cavort among
the swaying
reeds;
you forget your
world is a sphere
within another,
a shared quantum
riding a posit
of perception.

Potemkin Shifts

A smudged notebook
found in a drawer
names and numbers
scribbled together
raise a flicker;
the pages
tie our
potemkin shifts,
our tattered
odd continuing
together.

Magister Ludi

Quantifying
over sorts of
high importance
to structure
scraps of talk,
he flicks the
world in place
where it
rests
until
dislodged by a
logician's quip.

Rabbit

White half wild
thing sitting just
in from the bushes
peers unblinking –
a shooting gallery
cardboard cutout
that fits too
nicely into words,
a checkerboard to
play on inside
our private club
cut off from the
dirt he sits on;
the wide eyes
reproach.

Orchard

Strange to find
fruit and foliage
of one battle cloth
hiding each other
to delay the fall;
so when the tree was
picked and the few pears
patched rough
like buried bronze
were ranged
till winter to release
their worth,
the shelves seemed bare;
then after a frost to pick the
neighbouring medlars,
themselves disguised in
amber, there, crowning
the stripped branches
hung the clusters
forsaken, quizzical.

Shuksan

The mass builds from the
valley floor, dull igneous rock
crosshatched white, filling
grim holds; the walls lead
up from spire to spire
until the cloud line marks
the interval. Then the green
curtain rises to a stately
flow creased and folded
up to the wispy sky. No
fractious dolomite crested in showy
parapets tops the performance;
but cradled between
the outcrops of our core
a serene parabola
where a child might play.

Tulip Tree
(*Native to North America*)

Obtuse angle on the sidewalk
schoolroom overlap on the
trod foliage — the open top of
the single leaf now evidence
against the whole kingdom,
against the acute maple, the
molded subtle oak, the
predictable plane
its blotched trunk distant —
daring the cleancut invitation
to the muddy world. Staring,
waiting a reply on the ground
in the fall.

November Walk

Five ducks drift
in with the debris
worn brown sticks
on a wide grey sea
while sticks and ducks
drift in to shore
the sea sits on
a metaphor.

Snow Flurry

Dots of content
on chalk and wash
three ducks float by

Willow

A green wand snaps
A quiet follows
A friend is gone

Stickfigure

Piercing the past
to let bubbles
spill out
on to the page
I watch a
stickfigure
tip toe down
the binary way
left, right –
yes, no –
clothes go
and the form
itself.

Deep Forest Path

Is this the same
yellow violet
in the March moss?

Why! — here it is
in the leaves
of the book.

The Dinghy

The painter slips
loosening the dinghy;
for a moment or so
it bumps against the dock
then off a few feet
rocking in the waveslap
with the rope and its
pale sound limping after
it drifts out of reach;
as the distance widens
it slows, then sits
on the clean sea
watching the land
withdraw.